SCOTT FORESMAN
READING STREET

KINDERGARTEN

COMMON CORE ©

M000306655

Program Authors

Peter Afflerbach

Camille Blachowicz

Candy Dawson Boyd

Elena Izquierdo

Connie Juel

Edward Kame'enui

Donald Leu

Jeanne R. Paratore

P. David Pearson

Sam Sebesta

Deborah Simmons

Susan Watts Taffe

Alfred Tatum

Sharon Vaughn

Karen Kring Wixson

Glenview, Illinois

Boston, Massachusetts

Chandler, Arizona

Upper Saddle River, New Jersey

ALWAYS LEARNING

PEARSON

We dedicate Reading Street to
Peter Jovanovich.

His wisdom, courage,
and passion for education
are an inspiration to us all.

Acknowledgments appear on page 144, which constitutes an extension of this copyright page.

PEARSON

ISBN-13: 978-0-328-72437-6
ISBN-10:   0-328-72437-8
3 4 5 6 7 8 9 10 V011 16 15 14 13 12

Reading STREET

Dear Reader,

Wow! School has started! Did you know that we are about to take a trip along Reading Street? AlphaBuddy and your very own book, *My Skills Buddy,* will be with you for the whole trip.

Let's get ready. Pack your thinking caps. On Reading Street we will be busy learning to read and write and think. It will be hard work, but it will be fun.

You will meet lots of interesting characters. We'll make a stop in Trucktown too.

As AlphaBuddy likes to say, "Let's get this show on the road!"

Sincerely,
The Authors

All Together Now

 How do we live, work, and play together?

Week 1

Carol Roth
The Little School Bus
Illustrated by
Pamela Paparone

Big Book

Animal Fantasy · Social Studies
The Little School Bus by Carol Roth

Week 2

Unit 1 Contents

Week 5

Week 6

Don Leu
The Internet Guy

Right before our eyes, the nature of reading and learning is changing. The Internet and other technologies create new opportunities, new solutions, and new literacies. New reading comprehension skills are required online. They are increasingly important to our students and our society.

Those of us on the Reading Street team are here to help you on this new, and very exciting, journey.

See It!

- Big Question Video

- Concept Talk Video

- Envision It! Animations

- eReaders

Hear It!

- *Sing with Me* Animations

- eSelections

- Grammar Jammer

Adam and Kim play at the beach.

Concept Talk Video

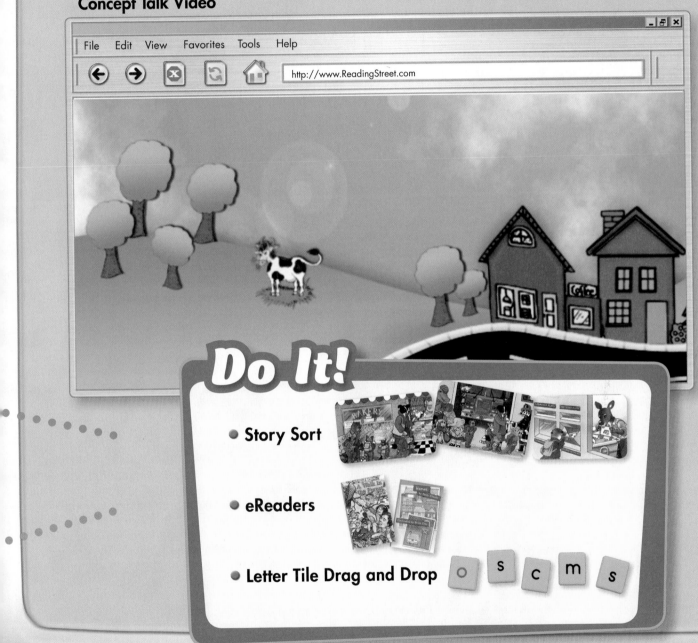

Do It!

- Story Sort

- eReaders

- Letter Tile Drag and Drop

9

All Together Now

THE BIG ?

How do we live, work, and play together?

Let's Listen for

Rhyming Words

Read Together

● Find things that rhyme.

■ What rhymes with *man?*
with *mop?* with *coat?*
with *book?*

▲ Which word pairs
rhyme: *nap/lap, cook/
coat, boat/goat?*

READING STREET ONLINE
BIG QUESTION VIDEO
www.ReadingStreet.com

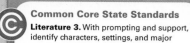

Common Core State Standards
Literature 3. With prompting and support, identify characters, settings, and major events in a story.

Comprehension

Envision It!

Literary Elements

READING STREET ONLINE
ENVISION IT! ANIMATIONS
www.ReadingStreet.com

Characters

Setting

14

Plot

Common Core State Standards
Foundational Skills 1.d. Recognize and name all upper- and lowercase letters of the alphabet. **Also Foundational Skills 3.c.**

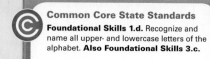

Envision It! | Letters to Know

Aa

Read Together

astronaut

Bb

baby

READING STREET ONLINE
ALPHABET CARDS
www.ReadingStreet.com

Print Awareness

Letter Recognition

Letters I Know

A a

B b

Words I Can Read

I

am

Sentences I Can Read

1. I am .

2. I am 😊 .

Common Core State Standards
Foundational Skills 4. Read emergent-reader texts with purpose and understanding.
Also Foundational Skills 1.a., 1.d., 3.c.

Phonics

I Can Read!

Decodable Reader

● Letter Recognition
Aa
Bb
Cc
Dd
Ee

■ High-Frequency Words
I
am

▲ Read the story.

READING STREET ONLINE
DECODABLE eREADERS
www.ReadingStreet.com

Who Am I?

Written by Bob Atkins
Illustrated by Yvette Pierre

Decodable Reader 1

I am Ann.

I am Ben.

I am Cam.

I am Dot.

I am Ed.

I am Emma.

I am Dad.

Common Core State Standards
Literature 2. With prompting and support, retell familiar stories, including key details.
Also Literature 1., 3.

Big Book

Envision It! Retell

READING STREET ONLINE
STORY SORT
www.ReadingStreet.com

Think, Talk, and Write

1. How do you get to school? Text to Self

2. Which is a character from *The Little School Bus?* Character

3. Look back and write.

Common Core State Standards

Speaking/Listening 1.a. Follow agreed-upon rules for discussions (e.g., listening to others and taking turns speaking about the topics and texts under discussion). **Also Language 6.**

Let's Learn It!

Vocabulary

- Talk about the pictures.
- Which do you use?

Listening and Speaking

- Point to the picture of the bus.
- Cover the picture of the bus with your hand.
- Pretend to drive a bus.

Vocabulary

Words for Transportation

bus

car

van

bike

Follow Directions

Be a good listener!

Common Core State Standards
Speaking/Listening 2. Confirm understanding of a text read aloud or information presented orally or through other media by asking and answering questions about key details and requesting clarification if something is not understood. **Also Literature 3.**

Let's Practice It!

Myth

- Listen to the myth.
- How does it begin?
- Who is King Midas?
- How does King Midas get the "golden touch"?
- What lesson does King Midas learn?

King Midas and the Golden Touch

Common Core State Standards
Foundational Skills 2.b. Count, pronounce, blend, and segment syllables in spoken words. **Also Foundational Skills 2.**

Phonological Awareness

Let's Listen for

Syllables

- Point to a picture, say the word, and clap for each part, or syllable, you hear.

- Which words have one part, or syllable?

▲ Which words have more than one part, or syllable?

Read Together

**READING STREET ONLINE
BIG QUESTION VIDEO
www.ReadingStreet.com**

Common Core State Standards

Literature 3. With prompting and support, identify characters, settings, and major events in a story.

Comprehension

Envision It!

Literary Elements

READING STREET ONLINE
ENVISION IT! ANIMATIONS
www.ReadingStreet.com

Characters

Setting

Plot

Common Core State Standards
Foundational Skills 1.d. Recognize and name all upper- and lowercase letters of the alphabet.
Also Foundational Skills 1.b., 3.c.

Envision It! | Letters to Know

Cc
cactus

Dd
dolphin

Ee
escalator

Ff
fountain

Gg
goose

Hh
helicopter

Ii
igloo

Print Awareness

Letter Recognition

Letters I Know

Read Together

Cc Dd Ee

Ff Gg Hh

Ii

cab

The cab is yellow.

Words I Can Read

I

am

Sentences I Can Read

1. I am .

2. Am I ?

Common Core State Standards
Foundational Skills 1.a. Follow words from left to right, top to bottom, and page by page.
Also Foundational Skills 1.d., 3.c., 4.

Phonics

I Can Read!

Decodable Reader

- Letter Recognition
  Ff
  Gg
  Hh
  Ii
  Jj
  Kk
  Ll

- High-Frequency Words
  I
  am

▲ Read the story.

Am I?

Written by George Helm
Illustrated by Tori Wheaton

Decodable Reader 2

I am Jan.

Am I Fran?

I am Len.

Am I Ken?

I am Kim.

Am I Hanna?

 I am Gus.

Common Core State Standards
Literature 2. With prompting and support, retell familiar stories, including key details. **Also Literature 1., 3.**

Envision It! | Retell

Big Book

Illustrated by Luciana Navarro Powell

READING STREET ONLINE
STORY SORT
www.ReadingStreet.com

Think, Talk, and Write

1. How do we work and play together? Text to Self

2. Where does the story *We Are So Proud!* take place?

Setting

3. Look back and write.

47

Let's Learn It!

Vocabulary

- ● What do you see that is red?

- ■ What do you see that is white?

- ▲ What do you see that is blue?

Listening and Speaking

- ● Where does the story take place?

- ■ What is your favorite part of the story? Why?

- ▲ Who is your favorite character in the story? Why?

Vocabulary

Color Words

red

blue

white

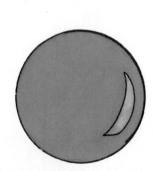

Respond to Literature
Drama

Carol Roth
The Little School Bus
Illustrated by
Pamela Paparone

Be a good speaker!

Common Core State Standards

Speaking/Listening 2. Confirm understanding of a text read aloud or information presented orally or through other media by asking and answering questions about key details and requesting clarification if something is not understood. **Also Informational Text 1., 2., 3., 7.**

Let's Practice It!

Expository Text

● Listen to the selection.

■ What is this selection about?

▲ How are the two flags alike? How are they different?

★ Why does the U.S. flag have 13 stripes?

♥ What do the 50 stars on the U.S. flag stand for?

The United States Flag

U.S. Flag Today

First U.S. Flag

Common Core State Standards
Foundational Skills 2.d. Isolate and
pronounce the initial, medial vowel, and
final sounds (phonemes) in three-phoneme
(consonant-vowel-consonant, or CVC) words.

Let's Listen for

Initial Sounds

● Point to something
that begins like *pig*.
Say the word. Say the
beginning sound.

■ Find other things in the
picture that begin like
pig. Say the words.

▲ Say these words: *pie,
pumpkin, pepper.* Do
they begin the same?
What about *pears,
cakes, apples?*

READING STREET ONLINE
BIG QUESTION VIDEO
www.ReadingStreet.com

Read
Together

Envision It!

Sequence

Common Core State Standards
Foundational Skills 1.d. Recognize and name all upper- and lowercase letters of the alphabet.
Also Foundational Skills 1.b., 3.c.

Envision It! | **Letters to Know**

Jj
jaguar

Kk
koala

Ll
lemon

Mm
motorcycle

Nn
nest

Oo
otter

Pp
penguin

Print Awareness

Letter Recognition

Letters I Know

Jj Kk Ll

Mm Nn

Oo Pp

mop

The mop is wet.

Words I Can Read

the

little

Sentences I Can Read

1. I am little.

2. I am the little .

Common Core State Standards
Foundational Skills 4. Read emergent-reader texts with purpose and understanding.
Also Foundational Skills 1.a., 1.d., 3.c.

Phonics

Decodable Reader 3

The Little Toys

Written by Roger Jons
Illustrated by Scott Salinski

 I am the little robot.

I am the little puzzle.

I am the little queen.

I am the little octopus.

 I am the little train.

I am the little block.

I am the little spaceship.

Big Book

Envision It! | Retell

1

2

3

4

5

Plaidypus
please return to
Grandma's house
112
Oak St.

6

Think, Talk, and Write

1. How do you help your family? Text to Self

2. What happens first in the story? What happens last?

Sequence

3. Look back and write.

Common Core State Standards
Foundational Skills 2.a. Recognize and produce rhyming words.
Also Language 5.a., 5.c.

Vocabulary

- Look around for squares and circles.
- Look around for triangles and rectangles.
- ▲ Which shape is your favorite?

Listening and Speaking

- Name the words that rhyme.

Words for Shapes

square

circle

triangle

rectangle

Listen for Rhyme and Rhythm

Be a good listener!

Get Ready For Grade 1

69

Let's Practice It!

Fable

- Listen to the fable.

- Why does the shepherd boy cry "Wolf!" the first two times?

- What lesson does the shepherd boy learn? Has anything like this ever happened to you? Tell about it.

- What do you think the shepherd boy might do next?

- A moral is a lesson learned. What new expression does this fable teach you?

The Boy Who Cried Wolf!

1

2

Common Core State Standards
Foundational Skills 2.d. Isolate and pronounce the initial, medial vowel, and final sounds (phonemes) in three-phoneme (consonant-vowel-consonant, or CVC) words. **Also Foundational Skills 2.e.**

Let's Listen for

Initial Sounds

Read Together

● Point to the pig in the puddle. Say "a pig in a puddle." What sound do you hear repeated?

■ Point to the man with the mouse. Say "a man with a mouse." What sound is repeated?

▲ Find things that begin with /b/, /d/, /k/, /p/, and /m/.

★ Name two things that begin like *ball*, *desk*, *key*, *pen*, and *met*.

READING STREET ONLINE
BIG QUESTION VIDEO
www.ReadingStreet.com

73

Envision It!

Classify and Categorize

READING STREET ONLINE
ENVISION IT! ANIMATIONS
www.ReadingStreet.com

Envision It! | **Letters to Know**

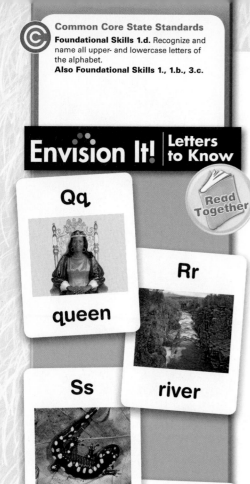

Qq
queen

Rr
river

Ss
salamander

Tt
turtle

Uu
umbrella

Vv
volcano

READING STREET ONLINE
ALPHABET CARDS
www.ReadingStreet.com

Print Awareness

Letter Recognition

Letters I Know

Qq Rr Ss

Tt Uu Vv

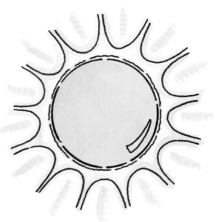

sun

The sun is hot.

Words I Can Read

the

little

Sentences I Can Read

1. Am I little?

2. I am the little .

Common Core State Standards
Foundational Skills 4. Read emergent-reader texts with purpose and understanding.
Also Foundational Skills 1.d., 3.c.

Phonics

I Can Read!

Decodable Reader

● Letter Recognition
Tt
Uu
Vv
Ww
Xx
Yy
Zz

■ High-Frequency Words
I
am
the
little

▲ Read the story.

At the Zoo

Written by Nitty Jones
Illustrated by Amy Sparks

Decodable Reader
4

I am the little walrus.

I am the little tiger.

I am the little yak.

I am the little ox.

I am the little rhino.

I am the little zebra.

I am the little umbrella bird.

Common Core State Standards
Literature 2. With prompting and support, retell familiar stories, including key details.
Also Literature 1.

Big Book

Envision It! | Retell

Think, Talk, and Write

1. Who helps in our town?

Text to World

2. Which things belong together?

↻ Classify and Categorize

3. Look back and write.

Let's Learn It!

Vocabulary

● Talk about the pictures.

■ Where do you go in your neighborhood?

Listening and Speaking

▲ What is your favorite color? Why do you like it?

Vocabulary

Location Words

library

park

school

post office

Tell About Me

Be a good speaker!

Curry Veggie Dip

Step 1

Let's Practice It!

Recipe

- Listen to the recipe.
- What is the third step in the recipe?
- Which words in the recipe name actions for you to do?
- Why do people read recipes?

Curry Powder

Step 2

Step 3

Step 4

Common Core State Standards
Foundational Skills 2.d. Isolate and pronounce the initial, medial vowel, and final sounds (phonemes) in three-phoneme (consonant-vowel-consonant, or CVC) words. **Also Foundational Skills 2.e.**

Phonemic Awareness

Let's Listen for

Initial Sounds

Read Together

● Point to the man in the ticket booth. Say "Man makes money." What sound do you hear at the beginning of those words?

▲ Find three things in the picture that begin with /m/.

★ Name other words that begin with /m/.

READING STREET ONLINE
BIG QUESTION VIDEO
www.ReadingStreet.com

92

Common Core State Standards
Literature 3. With prompting and support, identify characters, settings, and major events in a story.

Comprehension

Envision It!

Literary Elements

READING STREET ONLINE
ENVISION IT! ANIMATION
www.ReadingStreet.com

Characters

Setting

Plot

Common Core State Standards
Foundational Skills 1.d. Recognize and name all upper- and lowercase letters of the alphabet.
Also Foundational Skills 2.d., 3.c.

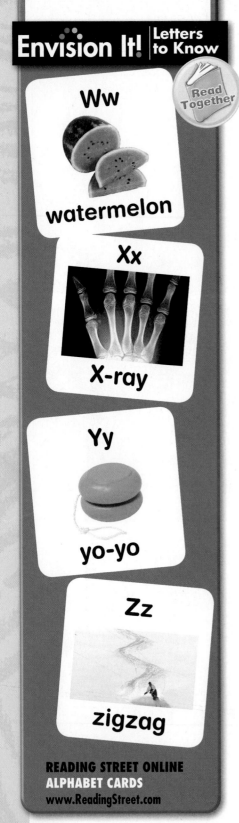

Envision It! Letters to Know

Read Together

Ww
watermelon

Xx
X-ray

Yy
yo-yo

Zz
zigzag

Print Awareness

Letter Recognition

Letters I Know

W w X x

Y y Z z

fox

The fox is red.

Words I Can Read

| to |

| a |

Sentences I Can Read

1. I am a  .

2. I to a .

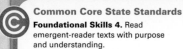

Common Core State Standards
Foundational Skills 4. Read emergent-reader texts with purpose and understanding.
Also Foundational Skills 1.d., 3.c.

Phonics

I Can Read!

Decodable Reader

- Consonant Mm (with rebus)
  monkey
  mule
  mouse
  minnow
  moth
  mole
  moose

- High-Frequency Words
  I
  am
  a
  little

▲ Read the story.

READING STREET ONLINE
DECODABLE eREADERS
www.ReadingStreet.com

Decodable Reader 5

Animal Friends

Written by Phil Morton
Illustrated by Julie Word

I am a little monkey.

I am a little mule.

I am a little mouse.

I am a little minnow.

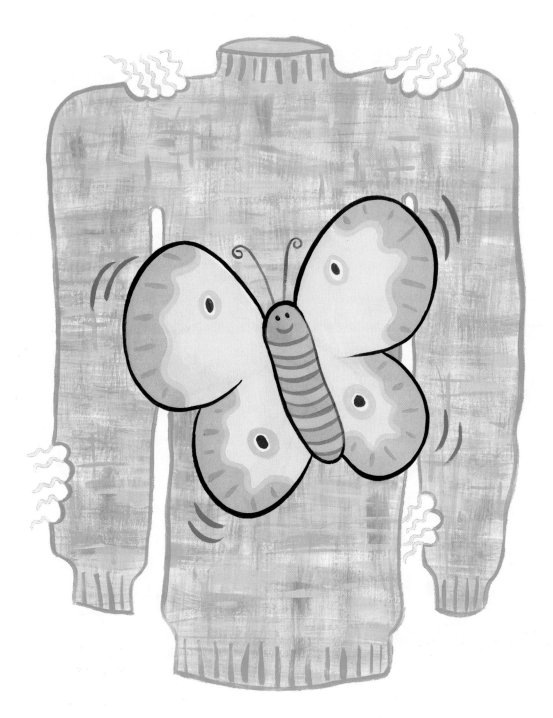

 I am a little moth.

I am a little mole.

I am a little moose.
Am I little?

Common Core State Standards

Literature 2. With prompting and support, retell familiar stories, including key details. **Also Literature 1., 3.**

Envision It! Retell

Big Book

Think, Talk, and Write

1. What do you do with your friends? Text to Self

2. Which is a character from *Smash! Crash!?* Character

3. Look back and write.

Common Core State Standards

Speaking/Listening 1.a. Follow agreed-upon rules for discussions (e.g., listening to others and taking turns speaking about the topics and texts under discussion). **Also Speaking/Listening 6., Language 6.**

Let's Learn It!

Vocabulary

- ● Talk about the pictures.
- ■ Put your hand up . . . now down.
- ▲ Put your hand in your pocket. Now take it out.

Listening and Speaking

- ● Make an announcement.
- ■ Listen to a classmate's message or announcement.
- ▲ Retell or summarize your classmate's message or announcement.

Vocabulary

Position Words

in

out

up

down

Announcements/Messages

Be a good speaker!

Common Core State Standards
Literature 1. With prompting and support, ask and answer questions about key details in a text. **Also Literature 3., 7.**

At a Farmer's Market

Let's Practice It!

Signs

- Listen to the selection.

- What is the selection about?

- Point to each sign. Tell what it means.

- Why does each stand at the market have a sign? Who will read the signs?

- How do the signs help Sandra with her plans?

Apples
10 for $ 1

Farmer's market

Common Core State Standards

Foundational Skills 2.d. Isolate and pronounce the initial, medial vowel, and final sounds (phonemes) in three-phoneme (consonant-vowel-consonant, or CVC) words. **Also Foundational Skills 2.e.**

Phonemic Awareness

Let's Listen for

Initial Sounds

Read Together

- Point to the table. Say, "two tan tables." What sound do you hear at the beginning of those words?

▲ Find three things in the picture that begin with /t/.

★ Name other words that begin with /t/.

READING STREET ONLINE
BIG QUESTION VIDEO
www.ReadingStreet.com

Common Core State Standards

Language 5.a. Sort common objects into categories (e.g., shapes, foods) to gain a sense of the concepts the categories represent.

Envision It!

Classify and Categorize

Mm

Read Together

motorcycle

Tt

turtle

Phonics

Initial *m*, Initial *t*

Letter Sounds I Know

M m   M m

T t   T t

Words I Can Read

to

a

Sentences I Can Read

1. I am a little .

2. I 🏃 to 🏫 .

Common Core State Standards
Foundational Skills 4. Read emergent-reader texts with purpose and understanding.
Also Foundational Skills 3.a., 3.c.

Phonics

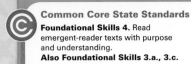

I Can Read!

Decodable Reader

● Consonant Tt
(with rebus)
tiger
turtle
turkey
toad
toucan
tadpole

■ High-Frequency Words
I
to
a

▲ Read the story.

READING STREET ONLINE
DECODABLE eREADERS
www.ReadingStreet.com

Decodable Reader 6

Let's Go

Written by Liz Cristie
Illustrated by Larry Jordon

I walk to a tiger.

I walk to a turtle.

 I walk to a turkey.

I walk to a toad.

I walk to a toucan.

I walk to a tadpole.

I walk home.

Envision It! Retell

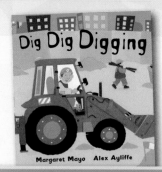

Big Book

READING STREET ONLINE
STORY SORT
www.ReadingStreet.com

126

Think, Talk, and Write

1. How are the trucks in *Smash! Crash!* and *Dig Dig Digging* different?

Text to Text

2. Which things belong together? ⟲ **Classify and Categorize**

3. Look back and write.

Common Core State Standards
Speaking/Listening 4. Describe familiar people, places, things, and events and, with prompting and support, provide additional detail. **Also Speaking/Listening 1.a., Language 5.a., 5.c., 6.**

Let's Learn It!

Vocabulary

- Talk about the pictures.
- What do you see that is big? What is little?
- ▲ Who is tall and who is short?

Listening and Speaking

- Where do AlphaBuddy's stories take place?

Vocabulary

Words for Sizes

big

little

tall

short

128

Respond to Literature
Drama

Be a good listener!

129

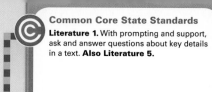

Common Core State Standards
Literature 1. With prompting and support, ask and answer questions about key details in a text. **Also Literature 5.**

Let's Practice It!

Folk Tale

● Listen to the folk tale.

■ What can you tell about the third little pig?

▲ What does the wolf say each time he comes to a house?

★ What lesson do the first two pigs learn?

♥ Why do people like to read or listen to this story?

The Three Little Pigs

1

2

130

131

Words for Things That Go

airplane

bike

truck

car

bus

van

boat

train

Words for Colors

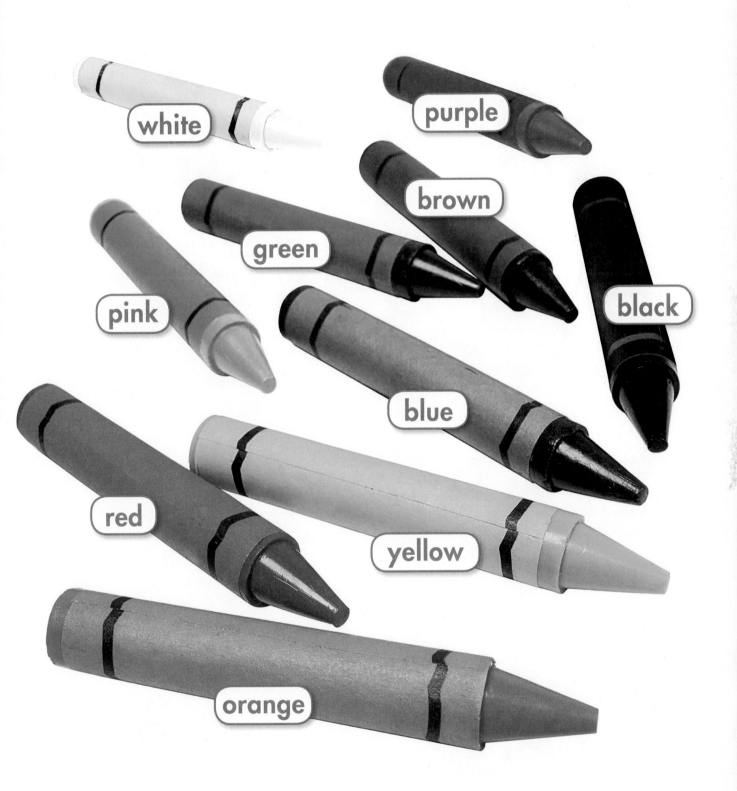

white

purple

brown

green

pink

black

blue

red

yellow

orange

Words for Shapes

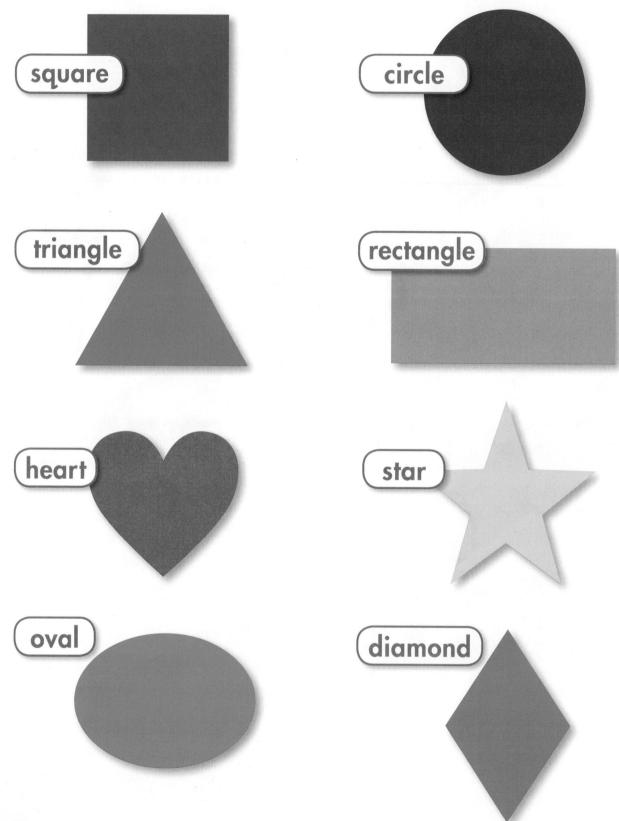

square

circle

triangle

rectangle

heart

star

oval

diamond

Words for Places

school
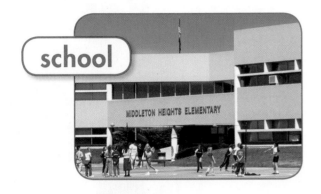

home

park

train station

police station

fire station

post office

library

Words for Animals

lion

mouse

puppy

dog

cat

duck

turtle

kitten

chick

hen

rooster

bird

136

butterfly

fish

whale

caterpillar

bear

panda

beaver

calf

cow

Words for Actions

skip

walk

run

fly

swim

ride

jump

hop

Position Words

up

down

in

out

on

around

over

under

My Classroom

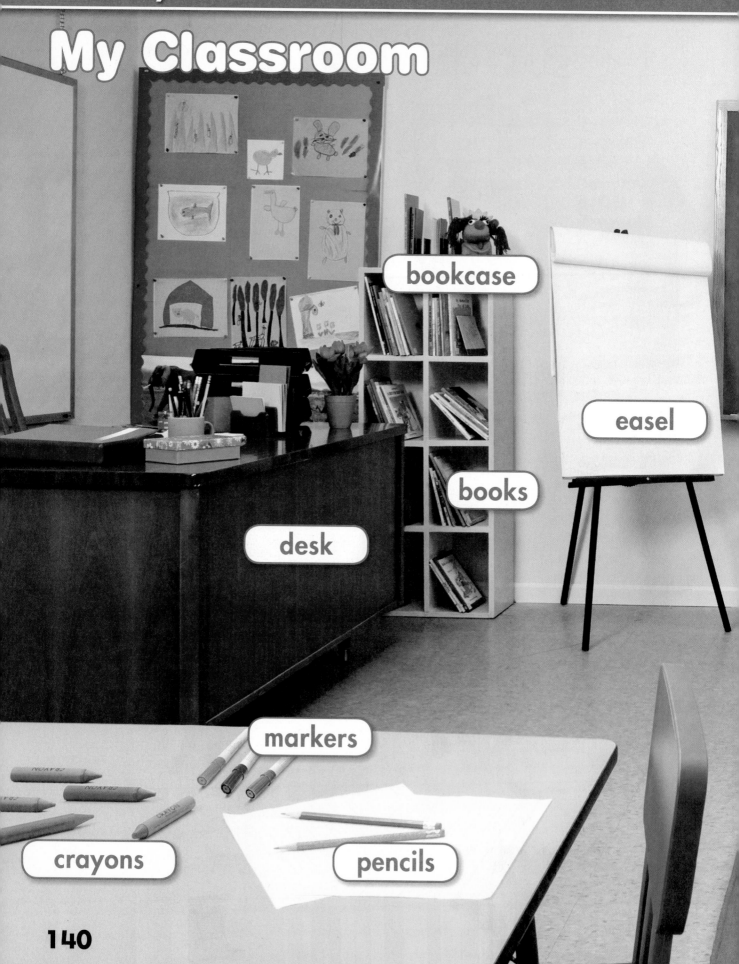

bookcase

easel

books

desk

markers

crayons

pencils

teacher

toys

paper

chair

blocks

table

rug

Words for Feelings

happy

frightened

worried

excited

angry

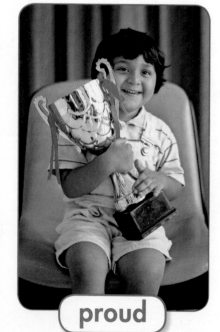

proud

sad

surprised

My Family

mom
mother

dad
father

sister

grandmother

grandfather

brother

Acknowledgments

Illustrations

Cover: Rob Hefferan

12 Manja Stojic

19–25 Maria Mola

30–31 C. B. Canga

32 Stephen Lewis

39–45 Cale Atkinson

48, 89, 108–110 Mick Reid

52 Ariel Pang

59–65 Natalia Vasquez

70–71 Akemi Gutierrez

72 Amanda Haley

79–85 Robbie Short

92 Ken Wilson Max

112 Jamie Smith

119–125 Dani Jones

130–131 John Ashton Golden

Photographs

Every effort has been made to secure permission and provide appropriate credit for photographic material. The publisher deeply regrets any omission and pledges to correct errors called to its attention in subsequent editions.

Unless otherwise acknowledged, all photographs are the property of Pearson Education, Inc.

Photo locators denoted as follows: Top (T), Center (C), Bottom (B), Left (L), Right (R), Background (Bkgd)

10 (B) ©Michael Keller/Corbis

16 GRIN/NASA

28 ©Drive Images/Alamy Images, ©Lew Robertson/Corbis, ©Motoring Picture Library/Alamy Images, Getty Images

29 ©Alan Schein Photography/Corbis, ©Ron Chapple/Corbis

36 ©Terie Rakke/Getty Images

56 ©Gerard Lacz/Animals Animals/Earth Scenes, Getty Images

76 ©G. Brad Lewis/Getty Images

86 (T, C) Jupiter Images

88 ©Andersen Ross/Blend Images/Corbis, ©Derrick Alderman/Alamy Images, ©Ellen Isaacs/Alamy Images, Corbis/Jupiter Images

96 ©Living Art Enterprises, LLC/Photo Researchers, Inc.

109 ©Jim Craigmyle/Corbis, ©Peter Christopher/Masterfile Corporation

116 ©Richard Stockton/PhotoLibrary Group, Inc. (BL) ©Tim Keatley/Alamy

127 (C) ©DK Images, (T) Getty Images

128 Corbis/Jupiter Images, Jupiter Images

129 ©ImageState/Alamy Images, ©Ron Buskirk/Alamy Images, Jupiter Images

132 (CR) ©Basement Stock/Alamy, (TR, TL, TC, BL) Getty Images

133 (B) Getty Images

135 (BCL) ©Guillen Photography/Alamy Images, (BCR) ©Kinn Deacon/Alamy Images, (BR) Flavio Beltran/Shutterstock, (TCR) Photos to Go/Photolibrary

136 (BR) ©Arthur Morris/Corbis, (CC) ©Cyril Laubscher/DK Images, (TL) ©Dave King/DK Images, (BC) ©Gordon Clayton/DK Images, (CR) ©Karl Shone/DK Images, (CL) ©Marc Henrie/DK Images, (TR) DK Images, (TC, BCL) Getty Images, (BL) Jane Burton/(c)DK Images

137 (CR) ©A. Ramey/PhotoEdit, ©Comstock Images/Jupiter Images, (CL) ©Cyndy Black/Robert Harding World Imagery, (CC) ©Dave King/DK Images, (BR, BC) ©Gordon Clayton/DK Images, ©Rudi Von Briel/PhotoEdit, (TC, BL) Getty Images

138 (TR) ©Rubberball Productions, (BR) Jupiter Images, (TL) Photodisc/Thinkstock/Getty Images, (BC) Photos to Go/Photolibrary, (TC) Steve Shott/©DK Images

139 (TR, TC) ©Max Oppenheim/Getty Images, (CR, BR) Getty Images, (C, BL) Rubberball Productions

142 (CR) ©Ellen B. Senisi, (BL) ©Simon Marcus/Corbis, (TR, TL) Getty Images, (TC) Jupiter Images, (C) Photos to Go/Photolibrary, (BR) Rubberball Productions